Approximate
Darling

Approximate Darling

POEMS BY

Lee Upton

Lee Upton (signature)

The University of Georgia Press

Athens and London

Published by the University of Georgia Press
Athens, Georgia 30602
© 1996 by Lee Upton
Designed by Betty Palmer McDaniel
Set in 11/13 Monotype Garamond
by Books International, Inc.
Printed and bound by Thomson-Shore, Inc.
The paper in this book meets the guidelines for
permanence and durability of the Committee on
Production Guidelines for Book Longevity of the
Council on Library Resources.

Printed in the United States of America

oo 99 98 97 96   P   5 4 3 2 1

Library of Congress Cataloging in Publication Data
Upton, Lee, 1953–
       Approximate darling : poems / by Lee Upton.
          p. cm. — (The contemporary poetry series)
       ISBN 0-8203-1811-6 (pbk. : alk. paper)
       I. Title. II. Series. III. Series: Contemporary
poetry series (University of Georgia Press).
PS3571.P46A86   1996
811'.54—dc20   95-36583

British Library Cataloging in Publication Data available

for my husband, Eric J. Ziolkowski

Acknowledgments

The author thanks the editors of the following magazines in which her poems, sometimes in different versions, originally appeared:

American Literary Review: "Personal History"
American Poetry Review: "Ocean Cave," "Psychic's Holiday"
American Voice: "Relentless Experiment," "Recitative"
Antioch Review: "Peripheral Matters"
Black Warrior Review: "The Fish House," "Herb Gatherers off I-80"
Boulevard: "Seaweed Soup"
Countermeasures: "Portraits of Nudes"
Cream City Review: "A Familiar"
Denver Quarterly: "Death of the Authors"
Epoch: "Contemporary Fragment (1)," "Woman in an Interior"
Field: "The Autobiographers," "Beatrix Potter," "The Brontës," "The Crossing of Orchids," "The Scarlet Letter," "The Visitation"
Hayden's Ferry Review: "The Rip in the Tapestry"
Iowa Review: "Gertrude to Hamlet"
Laurel Review: "Water Lily as Creation"
Massachusetts Review: "Milk-Glass Lamp in a Girl's Shape," *"The Virgin and Child with St. Anne and St. John the Baptist,"* "Women's Labors"
Missouri Review: "The Year of Our birth"
Northeast Corridor: "Rock Garden"
Ohio Poetry Review: "Alice Underground"
Ohio Review: "Summer's Customers"
Sycamore Review: "Brave Spirit," "A Tour"
Tampa Review: "Nympheum"
Visions International: "Puppet Play"

Contents

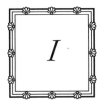

I

Peripheral Matters

Celestial objects
that wish to be flesh and bone,
winking through

a cobweb against the ear and eye:
We've followed you into parlors.
And in the lens

of each wet leaf—
the frowsy maidenhair,
and the fern that grows from a spout . . .

Wherever we wilt the leaves
we wind the fiddlehead tighter,
buckling throats.

Or we recline
upon the gills of an extravagance,
knowing by heart

whoever forgets us.
And for loss of any one mother
we make your trouble for you.

A letter can hardly hold us.
On page 158 another one of us
shall practice

dying inside her
parenthesis.
And a small fly,

alighting there,
must see through its wing
to our lacunae, and our exclusion.

The Brontës

For centuries, a chill soaks through stones.
Graveyards ray out from the suburbs
archaic as frock coats.

In any life one may discover
many doors that must not be opened.
Light chuckles in the pallets of ice,

and part of the city slides off below a hill,
a city translucent as egg white.
No matter a red room

and the tiniest handwriting.
No matter a flame at the roof of the mouth
if I cannot be ambitious with my heart.

The Hawk

To believe one is worth watching
beyond the haze of the basilica,
across the river and through

the pure gulfs of this air.
The mast of the day lifts over the river
where the hawk floats downward . . .

When will he unstitch
a stomach and heart?
How long a way it is

for him to be purposeful.
There are lines no one crosses
without shame, ours and theirs.

Power alights anywhere—
with a purpose that at last excludes us.

Nympheum

A scent of patchouli rises
where the water staircase descends,
where the trough of waterlilies
stagnates. For decades, the king's head
rests on a stair,

and one nymph,
her hand off at the wrist,
implores and implores.

In the afternoon's emulsion,
liquid and womanly,
we are new as mushrooms to them.
These women forever stand behind a spray.
As if the living must only stream before them.

Water is what their lives have become.
Like those with aspirations,
they gaze through a screen of fictions.

Trials

You can be tested or you can be savage.
You can request a quiet room
and a door that locks

whenever it closes. A rime
forms on the lights in town—
a rime to cut and deliver by hand

to your solitary desk.
Or you can remain savage.
Out of hills, out from under bridges,

out from the tower apartments—.
Although you find each night drawing forward,
the test awaiting the sudden door,

the rime of breath,
even joy with its breaking pain
or grief with its hands inside you.

The Ghosted Work

At the window, the sea draws birds
like brine flakes from a rock.
And in the pastures
the sluices of water run to the sea.

Near the pasture I pulled wild vines from firs,
stripping nooses,
as if I were pulling up carpeting.
And slowly in the midst of my work

it seemed I must be lifting a flap
of all living matter around me,
the emptiness almost rising into sight.
A fold of the sea lifted,

all of it twisting against
the tree line, rising and turning,
the light alive as flies,
the living sight peeled back

until I saw a walled carcass,
hair glued to a skull I loved,
swarms rising off the hinges of the skull.
I was stripping the choking vines from the firs

when a spirit's hand
halted me and made me speak:
If I owe you I want to pay you.
What is it that I owe you.

Woman in an Interior

Edouard Vuillard

Something of the snowflake,
the light reflected to the ceiling,

the scrubbed canal of the doorpost,
and the brush strokes outside the window . . .

It is all lit, in another way,
with the assaultive odor of peonies,

the dried iris,
the backlit curtain chord.

But we cannot enter entirely,
unheard of to take that honeyed

green vase,
the widebacked chairs dissolving,

the quickening carpet,
the glade of feeling

without pain or mortality
and uncentered—

to take a lattice made of
glances into a room,

a suggestion of what may
be enough, the flower arrangement

wild before this suggestion, this nuance
where no one may be seated.

The soft footfall
not far from us,

and all this territory
an interior of filaments

for the sparrow-sweatered woman.

The Rip in the Tapestry

When you put your hands through the slit of cloth
will you touch the horse's mane—
or feel the water where the birds dipped their wooden bills?
The visible knocked out by
gold traces, chains, jewels.

And in a moment will the woman turn to a sere flash,
a gold number, her skin, or a kind of gauze?
And now the horse's lips draw back.
The stem of a wrinkled
river, writhing upward into heaven.

Rent, lanced, bitten.
And I know why we must pause here,
hands hovering about the fabric as if it were a living throat.
This woman's husband will be put to death by the state.
Her gown of thread is a bell

that buckles where her husband clung to her legs.
Of course you too will pour your pearls
into the sea, you and
your darlings,
and your approximate darlings.

Relentless Experiment

How long before we become by degrees
aware? The diaphanous bag
with its bell-like bladders moves about,

and in the distant spaces
the white rock glistens with stables.
Curiosity is the mark

of our relentless experiment,
antechambers opening
onto antechambers and enfolded

fields of cabbage-headed glaciers.
When we motion toward another world,
the sides quake, the walls sway.

We arrive drench-eyed at the spot,
borne aloft into the gaze of our mother.
It is the wish to see her,

to flow into the little villa of her face,
that makes for our serious intention.

Lower Paradise

written, with gratitude, after reading Eavan Boland's poem of the underworld, "The Journey"

These that you see are real substances, assigned here for failure in their vows. Wherefore speak with them and hear and believe, for the true light that satisfies them does not suffer them to turn their steps aside from it.

                Dante, *Paradiso* (translated by Charles S. Singleton)

What is here of our own?
I asked the woman who appeared,
who had led so many to the first fountain of heaven.
Only by an accident of grace had my guide come to me

and then I could hardly look at her face.
What can we know of paradise and her circles?
Or I thought as much or perhaps the thought moved ahead
    of me
until I stood before a pool

startled suddenly by the faces hovering there.
The speechless mouth of a woman held me,
and my guide spoke:
She is a spirit who cannot kiss

the highest heaven.
See this nun whose vows were broken, a sister
abducted by ill fortune, her brother.
She keeps her glowing face here.

Then the pool's light filmed over with faces,
faces that are not like our own, each

entirely without sorrow,
even the humble, the poor in vows.

The faces floated and wavered.
For the longest time I looked upon the heavenly sister,
my heart for hers, uncloistered,
her word shattered.

This sister found her light
in heaven's lowest garden.
Above the gnawing of greed and the mill of envy.
Even in Paradise a power excludes certain hearts.

Even the beatific.
Broken-vowed, is it shame that bars paradise?
Here moved a spirit's shameless eyes and brow.
The waters were shaken.

My guide kissed my cheek,
and even now as I speak, everything dissolves,
the pure eyes, the calm pool and fountain.
How long had the world threaded its mist into a dream?

When I awakened, I was returned
to my own starless retreat—
and I sat up through the night
until a muslin of light

began to move across the window,
settling at last on all things alike.
Heaven hardly speaks to us now
unless it is traveling through the womb, our home.

How will we ascend to paradise?
How will we see the saints cluster like bees in God's
    honeycomb?

Here on this earth a split vow keeps us revolving
in no grade of heaven.

My own words are broken.
And yet how I wish to speak to her now,
that woman torn from her pledge by a violent hand.
What would I say to her other than

Beautiful sister, without a drop of blood,
you are forever in the slightest star, as we must suppose.
And yet how happy you are,
how simple is your heaven.

The Virgin and Child
with St. Anne and St. John the Baptist

restored after 1987 shotgun blast

What of the infinite work
in the bomb crater?
Scalpel marks and hatchings.
Is it enough
to be brought back
from extradition,
from dispersal,
from becoming a map under glass,
the crusted mountain range
and boiling ocean?
The raised blister of the right breast
in that art which is our politics,
our gold-dusted fruit.
If she is not to be a casualty,
the image must push up
through the needle pricks of space
as the conservator is
lifting the animal gelatins,
and we are falling—falling
between accounts,
between the factual, the minute
papers of a puzzle,
the cameras set up
for the dust settlements.
And I am seeing these women and their babies
as if something flits between the nerves of the eye.
But it is simple, a small thing,
the circle inside the circle inside the circle

of the dust filings
as the woman manifests herself.
Coming down the cliffside
I watch the cove rise into view:
the warmed stones,
rays leaping off the water, and it is
during this minute that the gallery explodes
a body,
the wound opposite the heart.
Not mine or yours,
but her image must be
the flesh's minister and emissary,
our contemporary.

A Familiar

Like a failure, foreshadowed.
Knife-boned.
Another mother unfurled.
Patience.
I was sitting up at night
to look inside her skull to coils of
balm
and then back into the lava cave,
whorled black sand and fire crusts.
Crawling toward the light I
touched—
For an instant I doubted her.
She is not a real
woman.
And then a horrible familiarity—
the meaning of her.
And now the past reassembles
its body, its round reflecting globe.
How will anyone know who she is
when seeing not her name,
but an agitation in the air.
A leprous mouth that cannot be cured.
And what may I make for her,
unbraiding no secrets,
to crawl down into the cave,
to draw her upright into the afternoon
as if she were
a giant eel wrapped in
parchment.
I am tapping on a wall,
a cliff.

I thought that I couldn't know her
or what separates us.
          And I look at my own body as if it is
a creature from some sea,
          half woman and half fish,
          and such thoughts must be for her
                resemblances
                          in lieu of her name.

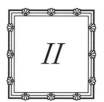

II

The Year of Our Birth

Wobbling through and making this little hut
on the outskirts of the city . . .

the outsiders float up
through lustrous antechambers—

until everything becomes newly visible:
the vistas through airplane windows,

the fields and the power plants.
It is the year of our birth

into one house where no one speaks—
next we are with the multiple people

opening our eyes in the dark
to their soft eyes and hair.

A tiara must remain
unbroken through the end of the century.

Gertrude to Hamlet

Inside, the turned liver,
the shiny capsules,
the taffeta

bladders and envelopes.
Would you divide
the anatomical

destinies of a heart?
I have no business
that is not a functioning

mystery to you,
a blooming peony
and a purse of tears.

Dust, ash
or nothingness,
what tears

in bursting waves,
ill-tempered stresses.
Say what you please

I am
up to my hands
in a split creature.

Which makes my body my own.
I live in it, I gather
my own into it. Otherwise,

who would you be,
beginning to be?
You wander my throne like measles.

Then Julia

Then Julia *let me wooe thee,*
Thus, thus to come unto me:
And when I shall meet
Thy silv'ry feet,
My soul Ile poure into thee.
Robert Herrick

My soul I'll pour into thee.
That oil I'll pour throughout you.
Whatever I would give you:
Some of my substance possibly—
I do not want to agree on an occasion

When this choir of jelly, this eternal float
Lying in its own sluice
Shudders out of the house,
Preferably to meet you—
Preferably where even

The linguists must hunger.
Julia's feet are wetted in silver.
The firmament soaks into her skin.
What dimple of distance must we trespass
To meet her!

Puppet Play

As they are sawdust, or wooden,
or hollow-hearted, as the drawbridge
of each mouth opens. As they are ours,
as we take them into our houses—
the mother with the rolling pin, the clown,

the crocodile with his pinhead tears.
As we are about to enter a miracle play.
Shadows climb a wall, stutter, and grow.
Whom have I made of cloth and wood?
Who shrinks me to a doorway?

Contemporary Fragment (I)

One leg and the torso,
the testicles only,
but not tortured,

graceful at ease—
the fragment relaxed,
the good bones above the navel,

the navel exquisitely rounded,
the indentation of the stomach.
A ladder of stone below the elbows

as if torn with some violence
from the rough essential block,
tissue deadened.

Otherwise a body of happiness.

Contemporary Fragment (II)

Helen and Menelaos
fragment of cup,
attributed to Makron

1.

She is lifting her headdress of veins,
so many fine lines in her dress.
Yet her husband is a fragment, an arm, a leg.
No, it is her servant who has lifted one fold
of her veil. She is like her servant except for
a larger eye, a forward jutting chin.
She sees what she will do.
I would rather see her this way
than as no one,
than as a mirage.
She sees that her husband is shattered.
It is her drama, her knowledge.
She is about to cover her eyes above
the broken story,
the columns of her dress,
the wires and cuttings.
Her eye is enlarged to take this in,
one power for another.
She is working her will to an advantage.
Her heritage forever to open her eyes
wide with fascination.

2.

Her time begins with a wash of wind,
tongueless. Her enemies grubbing through

the papers of her forebears.
Until we see the raped woman

enlarged and amplified.

She is to be a mill of lines, a revue
of screens. What emerges

from a monster but beauty's symbolic bird?
About the room

the monsters of perspective turn.

Recitative

You cannot leave your house,
Even if first you knock out the boards above your head.
These days when the leaves unfold:
To have one face, one body, one life—the recognition
Accompanies you

As if you wish to come upon your life again
In another way,
Stickily faced
With the raw cobra mouth of each day.

Across the parking lot,
The night fuzzes over
With loud speakers from the mall.
You cannot leave or pity anyone.
No one can pay you what they owe.

Your color changes the way
Water might suddenly move
Into the pores of this paper.
Impersonations of trackless stars

Cannot appall you.
And if the spoon of your god rises,
How can you be harmed?
You are circling away from my heart.
Your body is seamless and perfectly washed.

You will not come back as a child—
Not even my own.
Nor can you leave yourself.

The Visitation

Amanita virosa,
white and capped,
or another house

and stalk,
the brocade of
Lepiota procera,

fur work,
or unfurled silk,
gown crepe,

mussels.
Coarse stone.
Chill wash. Fog.

I hadn't visited
your house.
I hadn't been

to your house
in months.
In a dream,

I would neglect
a coral,
a fin,

and a handhold.
An eyestalk,
snowmelt.

Snow-bodied, dew-
touched, finched.
Is it you—

spotted,
shy, with
resurrection pinnules . . . ?

Women's Labors

You might want to be amused at the work
that is never done—or at our most difficult
labor, our work soonest ended.

In some work we are with most women,
crossing a bridge in our labor.
You will forgive me if I resort to Homer.

When the master returns,
the handmaidens are ordered
to clean up after the dead suitors,

washing blood from the tables,
the blood and water running from their sponges.
And then a cable is drawn about their waists,

and they are lifted from the ground
to perish in a great bunch together.
Even Homer must have pitied them:

a knot of slaves who only yesterday
laughed, believing the master
would always be missing.

How could I not pity them more—
slaves no one will defend.
If you are a woman in labor

waves break at the spine,
and a giant cable is drawn about your body.
You are held in the air for a very long time.

At last, later, you may be—
as I was—handed a daughter.
And for hours it seems there are no gods to claim us.

It is an illusion of course. But
even after the bracelet is clamped
upon the infant's wrist,

it seems we belong to no one.
We are out of history's singular lens.
For hours we serve no state, no master.

Brave Spirit

The wildflowers dissolved near the path,
the sudden blossoms, paler
pinstripes and ladders of white. But one

trillium like a bright napkin on a table
spites the early summer.
Our neighbor, a young mother, slips

through days with her sky
of clouds, her fullest studies.
She believes we are more than one body,

and that we live with a spirit,
stretching wings over the city's parks.
It is not velocity or rest

he is after, laughter cracked
and distilled within
boles and fall winnowings.

Such mercury, freed, unravels
a frond, pining
for a lodestar, pining

to speak again in another form,
within the eye of a blossom
closing at dusk,

the mother's milk of another.
Or to stand outside,
voicing his distance,

his right to say anything at all.
To trespass. Cross me,
we say to this companion. Cross

my reason, my ways.

Sea Box

A child brings his own luck.

The gilding crusted upon its top,
the gilt mirror of the jeweled box
in which seaweed fanned upon a rock.
The mirror showed its face

crusted with the gilded seaweed.
A box of the sea
to carry with you in a desert.
Or if you wish

a sea box for the starfish,
his bluing hand.
The box where the woman and the child float
cast into the open sea.

The light sifts its coins into the box.
If you will go to sea with him,
any child is made of money.
He brings his own luck.

Personal History

We were wrong to believe
we hadn't begun early enough.
Everything was waiting,
and nothing was entirely lost,

not even the houses we thought
lost to sleep, not even
the discards of any dream.
We were where we should have been all along.

The wind clamped upon the two rivers
dazzling us, and if we failed
to speak of some secret we couldn't name,
some disaster in which we periodically

forgot ourselves—
what we did or did not do,
even our silences—
it took a long time for us to learn whose we were.

Everything had been waiting for us.

Second Life

Hadn't we planned our lives?
And hadn't they appeared before us otherwise?
Every day we feel our way through
curious and lively skins of light.

We are emerging from underwater,
tilting the tabletop corals,
floating from the lost sunken staterooms.
Until at last some part of us is no one's.

Even words hardly moisten our second life.

III

The Scarlet Letter

How merciful it is,
that bright fallen bridge.
How it stands in the way of sunlight
to lose itself through interrogation.

She is what she cannot see,
but her partner's disgust extends
to the debris blowing
across a scaffold.

Any interrogation requires a secret.
This is everyone's body.
You must learn your letters,
the bridge and the cane.

Sun and water.
Humiliation is nothing—
to be left alone, oddly, to be
otherwise—

to join no one—
for years later,
the smell of cold, dull apples,
the first letter.

The Crossing of Orchids

The walls hold the town
against the sea and its wastes,

the houses' faint tint
of green soap.

Stairs lead down
to the cloudy

pores of water,
the invisible ink

of a little empire.

What is there to do
but to spread myself

everywhere,
to hold rain

in a moment of flesh?
If I could resemble

a soul whisked up
through a fontanel.

A body halfway

out of a body.
Whereas one orchid

is a fan atop
an anemone.

An orchid as the spread wing
of the owlet moth,

the furies of silkworms,
the necks of bitterns, herons,

ibises. The mutant

Cattleya labiata:
the curved instep

intimate in its motion.
Perverse and broken-backed:

brushing
trifolded petals.

Here a stricken body
rises to the surface,

a white carp

breathing an air
of parachute fibers.

Disappearing, the body
is a tendril,

speechless, annunciatory.
Yet would it matter,

returning,
anyone's eyes having seen

even one of us here?
A monster

warming the air

in which it is
jerked by a tiny branch?

Botanies

That fertile botany:
tropical, blousy
in your century.
One expected a dampness,
fallopian, in the
spayed cupworks.
Within the cooler chambers,
the mosses rested
in springy
underworld follicles:
Expatriates moved
back into their beds at night.
Sleepless,
unimpressionable,
returning to themselves
after any event.
Anonymous to power.

Portraits of Nudes

1.

Upon a wingbeat one spirit
is boisterous, not loathing us
from a corner of the frame.

As if we too traveled
in the sunlight
of branches, of vines,

our minds passing through
the portrait of a nude
and wishing to make her stand,

to open the curtain behind her.
Yet if the nude were to rise
how would she appear?

Levitations of flesh.
A terror.
As if fate were

an intelligence,
a surveillance
of the eyes in our faces.

2.

The secret of gardening
in a glass bottle
is to create vistas.

A pebble becomes a boulder
wetted with dew.
To see if moss will live

in its velvet
antlers—
and something fernlike.

The secret of gardening
in such places
commands forgetfulness.

Once begun, once ended.
Hardly rooted
in a handful of dirt.

The glass garden breathes
its stream
into the shady day—

until we no longer care
for stories about new lovers.
They live on one another's breath

in the same small spaces.

3.

We had waited at the dock for an hour,
and then we were waiting inside the boat at the dock
for a cruise to see the fjords.
The light was bright,
the air cool,
the effect what we call sparkling.
Until slats of darkness paused above the water,

the light between them.
The boat was starting when
I was fainting or half-fainting.
I was going under—five months into my pregnancy.
At the hospital the doctor
looked at the front of my black jumper
as if he saw a box camera's cloth and the future
blinking out.
But the baby proved alive, a pilgrim
with her own secrets
distant from our understanding.
She was as difficult to possess
as an arm of the sea.
Even then I knew that a form awaits her.
If she could only float
around such an immaculate shape,
the wearing of which is a special cloak
making her soul invisible to herself.

4.

Swaying and opening out to the overcast sky,
each water lily having exactly nothing to do
with the upturned face of a nude.

This field where the same plant grows itself again and again.
The pond that stretches to five acres,
a home to part from,

a muscular home.
Beyond the past with its curly fins,
its pearly orchidaceous flies.

5

The kettle dragon is curled like a foetus
but springs alert on the spout.
The child will spend hours in her pantomime,
running her fingers over the kettle's ribs,
the weft of rough edges.
She will learn
how anger lashes in waves and foams
until it becomes, if she is lucky,
clear and pure and useful—
as if any emotion is useful—
withdrawing from the roof of a small house.
The kettle's dragon rears forward,
unwrinkling its folds.
The dragon must be slain by a stranger
who will take her captive.
How would she have known
what it would be
to enter the dragon's throat,
the power of
her own dragon's body?

6.

From the airplane I see firefighters' foam
flooded over a row of houses in a suburb.

The child in me is traveling downward,
pulling herself toward our world

endlessly.
Like the silk worm, she will make means for a rich cloth.

7

Cold to the men
but pliable before girls and women.
He sat at the piano,

flop-headed, mossy with gin.
A man who can't stand men, he stood
only for the youngest women.

And there he was in the grape arbor
where the wealthy were pigeons to him.
Next he stood in the dog cemetery,

generations of dead dogs and their markers.
We couldn't get lost in the woods without him,
girls running over dog bones to a path of chicory.

We were caught in a gale,
clouds marbleized and split,
and the wind swept on our skin

a tonic. Every time we scattered from him
he was amused—as if he thought
this was what should happen to him.

Misfortune to chase the muses in a dog cemetery.
Of course it was in another age and the man is not dead,
and there is hardly enough malice left in me to remember

what art could not do for him.
The spirit of a border collie is upon me, girls,
he said—a line which illuminated him for a moment.

Perfect art is blind and strange, he said,
the excitement of it anyway—.
Did he think he was a satyr racing naked on an urn?
Even we knew he preferred girls to women.
With or without him we could get lost in the woods.
But luck was on our side:

Part of us was the oldest woman alive.

8.

We picked up the magazine at the side of the road
and our instinct: We should
bring this to our mother
who took it,
and, as we sat on the other side of the room,
flipped through the pages
and gasped
I'd never do that
I'd never do that
and then shuddering
took it out to the burn barrel
as if she had found a rat
in the closet,
its tail dripping out of a suit pocket.

9.

The brush strokes occupy me,
tell a distance.
The mill of making, her
outstretched arms.
Where do the eyes go?
It's the eyes all along the flank of her,
never in one place,
but knots in the air,

waving, rushing up,
the eye as a kind of mouth
but everywhere on her body,
seeing upon each of us
a particle of living dust.

10.

In our yard we may put a hand and a wrist
inside the trunk of the sycamore
as if a spirit blocked there
had broken her way out. There are feelings
about on the lawn,
intelligences, agitations.
Soon we will think of spring, of freshwater,
a sea breeze that moves inland.
Yet why does a green silk stay in our minds,
poured upon flesh, a font of green,
each stem of rainwater?
I am making my way through
the walls of a green wedding dress,
the stations, the minute stairs.
Her green gown, the navel pronounced.
Who begins like the font and ends
without a protest, as if even now
she would step under her wedding dress,
raise her arms, and pull it over her head?

Herb Gatherers off I-80

For those women in parkas:
wetness and tied leaves.
Who thrives
like the blackberry lily
or the rosemary willow?
In the greenhouse
thickened and warm with exhalations
they want for the body
some simple providence
of lemon verbena or the murderer's herb,
the suicide's rue,
all that is structured from within.
It is a search for a property
bedded in loamy mists,
like Ophelia pausing
until a leaf is the body's duplicate,
the drained and knotted malignancies
overlit by sea spawn
and spot-confused as the mind
who would repeat her body in living things.

The Shrine

I.

Not even for so much
as a much of a muchness
would that man let his eyes light his head.

He was dead at the top and alive at the root.
He was a man in a treacle-well,

and you will never draw him up again.
Nor can three sisters or two or one.
If you should be lowered to him,

you'll find him supping on a pig joint
and a trickle of jam.
And you will swing idly in your bucket,

an unnecessary thing,
like the poisonous leaves of the pie plant.

2.

But you're so harsh; you have few secrets.
When I slept in the room with nothing on the walls
I meant to be reticent about travel,

having been bred to facts and injunctions.
But you have such favorites; so few secrets.
And what can it matter, your outpourings,

56

if you are so harsh when you have such favorites.
Now there are two madonnas over my mantle,
their downpouring faces,

interiors shining with caverns.
What do they see in the earth?
Their velvety Polish shadings.

But you are harsh; you have few secrets.

3.

Ambitious, gut shaking,
smashingly various,
astute at the lip of the trough.
Whatever we are,
the fates know nothing of our empery of feeling.
If I am a diffuse wanderer,
a hormone-pitched mother,
of if I am quiet as a frond in moss,
I must be opening my mouth
to the imperturbable fates,
each with her silky ribbon,
her spool and needle in the breasts of women.

4.

Do you have a shrine,
a stranger, Danish, asked me.
If your house were burning, he asked,

what would you save?
Not a person but a thing.

And I extended my hand to the melancholy Dane
to force a conclusion.

What to save or carry, what to run with,
what shrine—
we fortunate ones.

Rock Garden

All summer the berries give off
new fragrances, and by morning
the sides of rocks glisten like
emery boards. Sunlight warps
the bed of Krishna-blue mussels.

Our window looks out upon
the courtyard's rock garden.
For hours, a fly dampens his feet
at the sill. Wherever we look
the color of the earlier moment

appears, now the yellow of the
dresser upon a husk of leaves—
as if the eye too needs a doubling,
an exposure, the unsettled
life as it settles.

Moistness clinging to us,
the way egg white clings
to a little bit of shell.

Summer's Customers

1.

Barberry and bunchberry and
the bittersweet nightshade,
yaupon and winterberry,
crab's eye

a member of the pea family
one seed of which leads to death.
Which berries may be poisonous,
which may thwart the devil's tongue?

This waxy beauty,
edible or inedible,
suns near the cold pond
where the cattle wade.

Here is your counter spell,
the seed on the tongue.
What we did
or what we should have done.

2.

The work that is done in a solitary mine
without regard to paranoid chance,
the work beginning without a sign,
deepening into whatever we cannot avoid.

No solvents, but the moment coiled.
Something chooses us and we too must

choose each morning, each day's alloy.
Who is it, then, that we distrust?

What discretions are required?
Whom shall we avoid?
As if everyone had the time or grace to shine
a light upon us.

3.

When the spring brings its customers,
turning upon the delicate, queerly
ephemeral days, complaining becomes a form
of conversation, a way we keep one another
pleasant and homely. Where the bee sucks there suck I.
Hardly. Nevertheless, to have spoken sometimes
proves useful and good.

4.

Green flowers are seldom appreciated.
The smooth Solomon's seal
and Indian cucumber root,
the greenfly orchid

and the water pennywort.
The common plantain.

The slender glasswort
speared and clustered as coral.
However shapely, these flowers are
barely discernible. They do not

draw the human eye to nick at
the breeze around them.
They build a green pantheon of heads.
They bow to a cooler judge.

Water Lily as Creation

To lie on the water
    like the water,
        gold and open, filamented,

caught and thickened
    into these
        gluey strands

floating above a vein,
    rising somewhat upon
        a pouring of oil,

a long umbilicus
    certain to cover
        the pond, to cup strands,

an image without suffering
    despite the tear-mark,
        the black poison glove

blotting a cup,
    a declension
        for God's daughter.

Alice Underground

With surely a liking
for delicate things—
a desire to scatter.

To push the girl through the keyhole,
attend to duties, dispatch,
render the image to be tinted

by an exquisite colorist.
In the doggerel of wakefulness
to riddle the hours

for which the girl stands
as witness, as courier
to the narrow island of logic,

she herself being impossible
to know in the ghost
bloat of a body.

The question is: Who must
fall, the telltale
blood on her apron?

Who must be a queen of shriveling,
a signature,
a happy grief?

The crockery is coming up through the garden.
A fish pond once inlaid on the lawn,
red glittery lit spawn and net and now
the fish pond is coming up through the garden.

The white chalk mushroom in the shape of a teaspoon.
The Victorians, their ponds,

their ivory fans,
a trellis carved into a fragment of elephant tusk.
Like the work of the writer
who must inscribe to the bone
each character, however young.
A small thing
with a great death behind it.

Milk-Glass Lamp in a Girl's Shape

Of course no hair, no skin can match her,
but the woven dress is a familiar ghost,
tattery as an old book,
tea-stained, moth-riddled.

You could better mend a lily
than dress her wholly again.
Beneath her gown
she's wire and a bulb—

its antennae quivering.
As if there came to this port
the secrets
now nearly a century gone

of light tipping through
the flesh,
dumb as a cell of honey.
She's without any sense

of distance
or amplitude.
I traced out the chord,
a corolla of furs,

before I could think:
not even a dumb thing escapes her time.
Over the years she has
herself become murderous.

Fidelities

Hepatica, columbine, shooting star,
What of the fidelities not mastered by fear?
The whalebacks of the garbage scows

Shudder across the morning bay.
Each day of the new year settles into place,
The nervous system of roots within a cliff.

A glass of juice beats on a saucer
Above the city's liver-colored skin.
Queerly figured in sunlight,

The balcony's rim rises above
Hepatica, columbine, shooting star.

The Repressed Island

Why should we go to the island
forever with its souvenir
shops of pottery and rugs?
Why take the mail boat

for outcroppings of rocks,
to trudge to a cottage
and the salty, star-lit lettuce patch?
The walls hold up without trauma

the ripe olive moles of weather.
There, in one copse,
the paring of a church,
the dikeworks of blunt grasses.

In the yard across from the bay
sea flocks pull out recklessly.
The past hardly happens to us.
Please do not start with tragedy.

Beatrix Potter

She is mopping about—she is moping
with a distrust, a revulsion toward weeping.
The dogs are eating the duck's eggs,

her privacy, her secret start.
Who would have the heart to say so?
Who would shudder with such directions

for children?
Your eggs will be found out,
your darlings.

Your plans will be cracked.
And we can laugh at a duck,
at a particularly stupid bonnet.

The foolish put on this show—
for us. Who must watch
their failures,

their disappointments,
their errors.
The charm of being poor at what one is,

luckless and silly.

Seductive Failures

Whenever the door opens
light sobs and gasps, and yet
the morning's voice is water-spotted
with forsythia breaking
into fine damp paper.
Already the scrolled shells
trouble a fountain,
trouble the trident-veined
arms of the horseman.
So why not at last admit
a great difference between us?
The morning flattens and extends
if there is no one for whom
our failures can matter.
Ice calved from the glacier,
currents of sand,
the glacier track breaking
against the bright mica.
Yet to once again fathom
the tiny suck in seduction
fails millions of us.
Even so much as that.

The Autobiographers

Something must happen.
It happened when you were there
or nearby or you

stopped on the side of the road.
A birthday,
date of first,

and second and third chances,
date of lost chances.
Or the spasms of history

become the spasms in our backs.
Yet who has lived enough
to know enough

to keep her mouth shut?
His mouth too.
Stories nest within stories

like egg cups.
Less mattering more
or more mattering—

Someone drowsy feeds us
toast and butter.
Earlier, someone's light

skips through a room.
And in the womb,
she is a lovely minnow.

Ocean Cave

When the cannon flash of a wave
strikes at the wall deep in the cave
a woman's voice comes back—
a woman visited by an engine
or a dragon. Even under

the pines on the cliff,
knobby pines, dwarfed in the wind,
my memory wishes to leave my mind like a tide.
I listen for the woman broken apart
into skimmings, floating out to the deep waters.

A voice without a body now
locked there by her witch.
Her voice is broken again into a breathy cry.

Listening, I have my big infant daughter on my lap.
The two of us rest high above the cave mouths.
When we hear the concussion of the wave—
the woman's cry—
how can I account for my strangely perverse joy?

I pay Caesar Caesar.
I worship perishable skin.

Psychic's Holiday

The two teenagers wrestled on the high deck
until the man flung himself past them
(a dancer, I recognized later,
from the floor show).
The teenagers shrugged back from the rail
and the man stood
in the briny drifts of air (it was after midnight)
and standing seemed to be
his pure and undisputed discipline.
I was thinking then of a glass case in the ferry's lounge
and the chopping block of coral
streaked like a horse's hoof there.
But then the silvery particles of air
puckered into an event around the man's head,
and I could do nothing but see
how he would lower this boat's guillotine
upon his private ocean.
Once he had been a widower
stepping on a cigarette beside a hearse.
In the next life
he will repeat himself to become
a woman corrupting herself with loneliness.

The Fish House

A smell of ammonia or aluminum
and you're here.
You've entered at the side door.

The place seems beaten with a mallet.
A cathedral fish
with weeping gills loiters

among bright things stuck in ice.
And the young person you had been
blinks at a table.

What have we learned since we sat
in just that position, leaning forward?
Now we know enough to leave?

Just saying so can't make that woman
stand from the table,
sick of betraying herself or anyone.

Tell her what we can.
The past is a fish
that cannot swim.

It is mounted on a wall
above a woman's head.
She does not have to admire it.

Seaweed Soup

The dried seaweed
is a museum piece,
a garland of rags.

But in a bowl of hot water
no longer can it be
the flayed dried ribbon

of a burial
but a tip of the sea's tongue.
No longer something of soot,

an artifact from a
burning building—
but greenery

with a parasite's tenacity
in the undertow,
coming adrift with

the light skiff work
of a lesion.
We make a floating garden

in a clear soup,
sinews filling
with the tea of it.

We have also consumed
tiny dried silvery fish,
once desiccated in a basket.

Until we too are in a sea,
drawn to a surface
boiling with emblems.

A Tour

We will tour the Springs and the Baths and the Gardens . . .
                                                    a letter from a friend

And the pitcher's thistle and hoary puccoon,
bluestem and riverbank grape and

marrum grass, the red osier
dogwood by the chokeberry,

and the stands of pink willows.
But first we sit in folding chairs

until I rise to talk to my friend,
and already we are breaking my promises,

and it is beginning, our errors.
The red pears hung

cold-skinned on the trees,
and the deer stepped

among the grapevines.
We clapped our hands and still they wouldn't run from us.

There must always be at least two women
who will clap their wings

over a dinner table to set
the clouds startling from the lake.

The women last. They're friends.
But the men do not return to the table again.

Nevertheless, how good it will be
to tour the springs and the baths and the gardens,

the late afternoon as cool and misted
as the skin of a grape.

Why would we want other afternoons,
now that we are so calm, so serious?

Needlework

The thread is crimped—oh
jeweled everlasting—
the quick puncture.
A leafy mass of knots,

speechless and perfect,
cannot cover
a face slashed or
the thread drawn

through the base
of a garden.
A rainy sedge
latches and pulls

into matter.
And now nightly
it suits us
to unravel our names—

as if we trusted them
lightly
with our barely
discernible plots

to cover our naked
anonymous bodies.

Death of the Authors

The root of anger refers
to the throat's closing,
a clamping and inflammation.

To make what we have
simply from the rootstalk
of the throat—.

The cold drops of rain
depend lightly
within their perfections

as if the roots in their miniature life
must be fed by air now.
An ancestor,

heavy with thirty years of her death,
pooling her heartless ink
within another woman's wrist.

2.

Virgo Lactans
from a Book of Hours

If death wishes to work up from the pages,
a child must ride upon the sea
of her mother's blue robe,

82

swelling from the heavens into the earth,
illuminating at odd moments
with a faint incalculable lamp.

If where we begin is the living body,
death dries his skin
nearby. Lipless, without mercy.

As if only a full mouth would give him a memory.
Just as the author must open her eyes to him
and put on his skin and night-torch.

3.

*She pasted away
printer's error*

Her words were paste for paper.
When the impulse came to purify,

to beat the hail from her pages,
her hands fled to another sphere.

She was a paste on her day.
Her words were paste for paper.

She pasted away.

4.

What I recall best:
a sweet and sour fish
stiffened on a black platter,
its eyes glazed over

with crenellations of dust.
Next booth: fillets laid out

like wrist watches.
By midafternoon,
an oily shell pattern.

Another afternoon in another city:
spare ribs brushed
with a whisk dipped

in what looked like lacquer.
And around the corner
a flavorful lichen appeared

at a stand, tended,
as it turned out,
by one refugee.

To what would the author
compare this fragrance?
Her mind rising earnestly

within the obdurate fact
of the colonies.

5.

When I stepped into the next century
how could I know
even so much as
the grief-work of iron falcons?
I was a scribbler without pardon.
The lampblack made runes
at the windows.

And I was practical with my mind,
knowing one corner of it at last
from long acquaintance.

6.

Spies, their questions were not innocent.
We know our enemies.
We think we can outwit them.

We had rooted at the lie,
At the haggish go-betweens of words.
Where were the tides and weathers,
The marble with its inexpressible message?

We know our enemies.
We think we can outwit them.
That struggle to form
The coppery arch of feeling.
The enemies of wit—to know them,

The spite in any heart.
How could they know themselves—
Our rivals—without our wit?

The light imposes.
The ransom of a word.
The lie and the secret.

In the dense forest the spies take root.
The institution lamps grow dim.
The mirror thickens with rivals.

7.

A lamp in the screenwriter's study sheds welts,
and like her assumed audience
she too begins to hate
the CEO/head of international research/
drug ring kingpin.
His death must be prolonged and
vaguely humorous,
before the buzzsaw, cement mixer, document shredder,
elevator shaft.

8.

How it might emerge naturally,
out of a hollow,
a running stream,
the eggs of the koi clinging there—
the pondweed,
willow moss,
water hyacinth,
frog bit,
mill-pond lily,
the Ophelia,
its umbilicus
the color of rhubarb
beneath pocked leaves,
the damp startled face.

9.
I rise with my red hair
And I eat men like air.
Sylvia Plath,
"Lady Lazarus"

And I, like men, eat air.
And men . . .

Like men and air—
with my red hair
I rise.
Eating men.
Reddened into hair.
Rising red.
Eating men rising into
air. Earth eats air.
Air eats men.
Reddened with hair.
Airs eats women and
men. I rise and rise.
Rise with my reddening hair.
Why should I
ever bother.

10.

She had arrived at a spike of palms,
her full skirt bundled close to her thighs.
She crouched toward the sound of wave suck
and then before the shadow of the body
of an unknown woman,
the arm caught in a lava nook and thus
leaving the trespasser breathless,
slithering backward.
And the trespasser's first impulse is to cry,
Pardon me. Please pardon me.

11.

Shortly before her death
she requests a mirror.
    Dickinson, #845:

Be Mine the Doom—
Sufficient Fame—
To perish in Her Hand!

That we may love her better
with our curious hunger.

The Contemporary Poetry Series
Edited by Paul Zimmer

Dannie Abse, *One-Legged on Ice*
Susan Astor, *Dame*
Gerald Barrax, *An Audience of One*
Tony Connor, *New and Selected Poems*
Franz Douskey, *Rowing Across the Dark*
Lynn Emanuel, *Hotel Fiesta*
John Engels, *Vivaldi in Early Fall*
John Engels, *Weather-Fear: New and Selected Poems, 1958–1982*
Brendan Galvin, *Atlantic Flyway*
Brendan Galvin, *Winter Oysters*
Michael Heffernan, *The Cry of Oliver Hardy*
Michael Heffernan, *To the Wreakers of Havoc*
Conrad Hilberry, *The Moon Seen as a Slice of Pineapple*
X. J. Kennedy, *Cross Ties*
Caroline Knox, *The House Party*
Gary Margolis, *The Day We Still Stand Here*
Michael Pettit, *American Light*
Bin Ramke, *White Monkeys*
J. W. Rivers, *Proud and on My Feet*
Laurie Sheck, *Amaranth*
Myra Sklarew, *The Science of Goodbyes*
Marcia Southwick, *The Night Won't Save Anyone*
Mary Swander, *Succession*
Bruce Weigl, *The Monkey Wars*
Paul Zarzyski, *The Make-Up of Ice*

The Contemporary Poetry Series
Edited by Bin Ramke

J. T. Barbarese, *New Science*
J. T. Barbarese, *Under the Blue Moon*
Scott Cairns, *Figures for the Ghost*
Scott Cairns, *The Translation of Babel*
Richard Chess, *Tekiah*